HOW I FEEL

by June Behrens

photographs by Vince Streano

AN ELK GROVE BOOK

 CHILDRENS PRESS, CHICAGO

Library of Congress Cataloging in Publication Data

Behrens, June.
  How I feel.

  SUMMARY: Children's expressions of their feelings
of love, anger, joy, and other emotions are reflected
in accompanying photographs.
  "An Elk Grove book."

  1. Emotions—Juvenile literature. [1. Emotions]
I. Streano, Vince, illus. II. Title.
BF561.B34   152.4   72-10188
ISBN 0-516-07618-3

3 4 5 6 7 8 9 10 11 12 13 14 15 16 17 18 19 20 21 22 23 24 25 R 75 74

To Pauline Brower

With special acknowledgement to
Mrs. Violet Carter, Principal,
and the staff and children at
Carson Street School
Carson, California

I am so proud to be the line leader.

I stand straight and tall and everyone

4

follows me.

I lead the way to the play yard.

Do you like to be the line leader?

Once I was mad at my sister.

I threw an apple core at her.

I hit her but I didn't mean to.

I didn't feel good about it.

6

Bunny likes to wiggle his nose.

He is soft and warm and I love him

better than anything.

What do you love best of all?

I like to paint pictures.

I can paint boats and white clouds.

10 My boats are the best in the class.

I feel good when my teacher

hangs them on the wall.

One of my friends hated me.

He threw sand at me.

12

Then he ran away.

I only hated him for a day or two.

I worry about cars.

They come by very fast.

14   I always look both ways.

When the crossing guard helps me,

I don't worry.

I get mad at Danny.

I tell him to go home.

16 When he is gone, I have no one

to play with.

Then I feel lonesome.

I'm sorry, too.

Sometimes my friend Roger

makes me mad.

18

I get so mad I want to hit him.

When I sock that tetherball hard,

I feel better.

Happy makes you want to jump

up and down.

You feel so good inside.

I am happy when I win the game.

When do you feel happy?

My sister always puts her clothes

on my bed.

I get mad and throw them on the floor.

We hate each other for a while.

Then we make up and play
with my card game.

My mother worries about me.

When I cut my finger, she fixes it.

She plays games with me

when I am sick in bed.

26

I start around on the rings.

My hands get all wet and slippery.

I can NEVER get all the way around!

But I keep on trying.

In summer I sleep in my tent in the yard.

Sometimes I am lonesome.

My dog Jake comes to bed with me.

Then I'm not lonesome any more.

28

I feel sorry for Bobby.

Big boys pick on him and take away his lunch box.

Sometimes he cries.

Then they are sorry, and they give it back to him.

I found a little red fire truck

in the front yard.

When my neighbor Mark came home,

32
he was mad.

That fire truck was his birthday present.

I felt bad because he thought

I took the truck on purpose.

My daddy likes to take me places.

Sometimes I go to the ball game with him.

He gets me ice cream.

I like him so much I really love him.

I like to dance with my sister.

She swings me around until I'm dizzy.

36

Then I get silly.

We laugh so hard we cry!

Sometimes I'm afraid in the dark.

I feel all alone.

38

I think about noises and things.

Everything is all right when my mom

kisses me good night.